HARVEST
RECIPES

compiled by
Carol Wilson

illustrated by
Wilfrid Ball RE
and other artists

SALMON

Index

Cover pictures *front:* Picking up the sheaves *by John MacWhirter*
back: A good days work *by Howard Walford*
title: Threshing *by Wilfrid Ball* RE

Printed and Published by J. Salmon Ltd., Sevenoaks, England © Copyright

Hasty Harvest Pudding

A popular country dish made to celebrate the start of harvesting.

Base :	**1 lb cooking apples, peeled, cored and sliced**
	1 oz butter 1 oz granulated sugar Grated rind of 1 lemon
Centre :	**1 oz butter 1 oz flour 15 fl oz milk**
	2 tablespoons granulated sugar 1 egg, beaten
Topping :	**2 oz Demerara sugar 1 teaspoon ground cinnamon**
	Butter to dot

Base: melt the butter in a pan and add the apples and sugar. Cook gently until soft, then remove from the heat and stir in the lemon rind. Put the mixture into a buttered $1\frac{1}{2}$ pint overproof dish.

Centre: melt the butter in a pan and stir in the flour. Cook gently for 2 minutes, stirring constantly and gradually blend in the milk. Bring to the boil, stirring and simmer for 2 minutes. Remove from the heat and beat in the sugar and egg, a little at a time. Return to the heat and cook for 1 minute, stirring all the time, then pour over the apples.

Topping: mix together the sugar and cinnamon and scatter over the pudding. Dot with butter and place under a hot grill until the sugar topping caramelises. Serve hot or cold. Serves 4-5.

Spring Ploughing *by Wilfrid Ball*

Bedfordshire Clanger

A pudding made for workers in the fields. It contains savoury ingredients at one end and fruit at the other - a complete meal in one long pasty.

Savoury Filling : 1 onion, chopped finely   1 tablespoon oil   8 oz minced pork
                   1 teaspoon mixed herbs   1 cooking apple   Salt and pepper
Sweet Filling :   2 eating apples   Grated rind and juice of 1 orange
                1 oz granulated sugar   4 oz dried fruit (sultanas, currants, dates, etc.)
Pastry :   12 oz self-raising flour   6 oz shredded suet   Pinch of salt

Savoury filling: Fry the onion in the oil until soft. Add the minced pork and herbs and cook for 5 minutes, stirring. Peel, core and chop the apple and add to the pan. Cook for another 5 minutes and season to taste. Leave to cool.

Sweet filling: Peel and chop the apples and mix with the grated orange rind and juice, the sugar and dried fruit.

The dough: Put the ingredients into a bowl and mix with enough cold water to form a firm dough. Roll out and cut two 10 inch circles. Roll out the trimmings and cut two 10 inch strips. Stand one across the centre of each circle and press lightly to form a wall. Put the pork filling close to one side and the sweet filling to the other. Bring up the edges and pinch together to form a pasty. Sprinkle 2 teatowels with flour and tie up each clanger, leaving enough room for them to expand. Put into a pan of boiling water and boil for 1 hour. Finally, dry off in a warm oven. Serves 2.

Chestnut Shortbreads

These soft, shortbread biscuits are golden brown with a spicy, nutty flavour.

6 oz chestnuts	**4 oz butter, softened**
¼ pt milk	**2 oz honey**
2 inch piece cinnamon stick	**1 teaspoon ground cinnamon**
6 oz wholemeal flour	

Set oven to 350°F or Mark 4. Skin the chestnuts by making a small slit in the skin, cover with boiling water and leave for 5 minutes. Peel off the outer and inner skins while still warm. Put the peeled nuts into a pan with the milk and cinnamon stick. Bring slowly to the boil and simmer, covered, for about 20 minutes until the milk is absorbed. Put the chestnuts into a mixing bowl and mash to a pulp. Beat the chopped butter with the chestnuts then mix in the honey and ground cinnamon. Fold in the flour and work, with the fingers, to make a soft dough. Turn out on to a floured surface and roll out to ¼ inch thickness. Cut out 2½ inch rounds with a cutter and lay on a floured baking sheet. Bake for 15 minutes until golden brown but still soft Transfer very carefully on to a wire rack to cool.

Blackberry Pie

There is nothing more redolent of Autumn than blackberries picked from the hedgerow and made into this succulent pie.

1 lb blackberries, rinsed and drained very well and any stalks removed

10 oz shortcrust pastry	**4 oz soft brown sugar**
½ level teaspoon ground	**A walnut of butter**
cinnamon or nutmeg	**1 tablespoon sherry**

Milk or beaten egg to glaze

Set oven to 400°F or Mark 6. Lightly butter a 10 inch pie plate. Roll out the pastry on a lightly floured surface and use half to line the pie plate. Layer the blackberries and the sugar blended with the spice, over the pastry base. Dot with the walnut of butter and then sprinkle over the sherry. Cover with the remaining pastry, trimming the edges and sealing well. Decorate with the pastry trimmings and make a small steam hole in the centre. Brush with a little milk or beaten egg to glaze and cook for about 30 to 35 minutes or until the pastry is golden. Serve hot with cream. Serves 4 - 6.

Harvest Pot

A farmhouse dish, typical of many all over Britain, which made use of lamb, mutton or pork. This recipe was especially popular in the Cambridge region.

8 oz dried haricot beans, soaked or 450g tin used straight from the tin

3 lb mutton or lamb, cut into chunks	**2 onions, sliced**
Oil for frying	**Salt and pepper**
2 rashers bacon, diced	**1 tablespoon Worcestershire sauce**

Set oven to 325°F or Mark 3. If using dried beans, soak in cold water overnight. Next day, drain the beans and place in a pan of fresh water. Bring to the boil and cook for 10 minutes. Strain the beans and reserve the liquor. If using tinned beans, strain and reserve the liquor. Heat the oil in a frying pan and brown the meat on all sides. Layer the meat, beans, bacon and onion in a large casserole, seasoning each layer with salt and pepper. Pour over the bean liquor, making up with water to cover, if necessary. Cover and cook for about 2 to 3 hours until the meat is tender. Stir in the Worcestershire sauce just before serving. Serves 5-6. Dried or tinned beans can be used but dried beans have a better flavour.

The Stackyard *by Wilfrid Ball*

Baked Stuffed Apples

An economical but delicious dessert.

4 large cooking apples	**1 teaspoon ground cinnamon**
3 oz butter	**4 oz raisins or sultanas**
4 oz dark soft brown sugar	**2 oz walnuts or hazelnuts, chopped**
	4 whole cloves

Set oven to 350ºF or Mark 4. Core the apples and with the point of a sharp knife mark a line around the centre of each, scoring through the skin. This ensures that the apples will not burst during cooking. Place the apples close together in a shallow, buttered baking dish. Cream together the butter, sugar and cinnamon and stir in the raisins or sultanas and nuts. Fill the centre of each apple with the filling (if there is too much place the surplus in the base of the baking dish) and top each with a clove. Bake for about 30 minutes until the apples are soft and fluffy. Serve hot with chilled cream or ice cream. Serves 4.

Lancashire Potato Cakes

Lancashire farm workers celebrated the potato harvest with a 'shutting' in the barn;
traditional songs were sung and a selection of potato dishes were enjoyed.

1 lb potatoes, peeled	**1 egg**
1 oz butter	**4 oz self-raising flour**
½ teaspoon salt	**1 teaspoon baking powder**

Boil and mash the potatoes. Stir in the rest of the ingredients to make a soft but not sticky dough. Roll out on a floured surface to ½ inch thickness and cut into rounds or triangles. Cook for 5 to 7 minutes on each side on a hot greased griddle or heavy frying pan, until golden brown. Serve immediately with plenty of butter.

High Summer *by Wilfrid Ball*

Fruit Tansy

Tansy was a popular harvest dish that originated in the 14th century. Originally it was a dish of eggs and herbs flavoured with tansy juice, but by the 17th century it had developed into a sweet pudding and the bitter tansy herb was omitted.

1 lb cooking apples or gooseberries	**4 oz granulated sugar**
	4 eggs, beaten
4 oz butter	**1 dessertspoon orange juice**
2 fl oz water	**4 oz fresh white breadcrumbs**

Top and tail the gooseberries or peel, core and slice the apples. Melt the butter in a pan with the water and add the fruit and sugar. Simmer until soft and leave to cool. Gradually beat in the eggs, followed by the orange juice. Place the pan over a low heat and add the breadcrumbs, a few at a time, stirring constantly, until the mixture thickens like a custard. The amount of crumbs needed will vary according to how juicy the fruit is; do not add too many or the mixture will be too dry. Serve at once with fresh cream. Serves 4.

Orchard Pork

A delicious way of cooking pork with autumn orchard fruits.

3 lb sparerib joint of pork	5 fl oz cider
1 teaspoon oil	Water or stock as needed
Salt	3 tablespoons flour
3 eating apples	2 tablespoons Calvados or cider
3 firm pears	2 tablespoons redcurrant jelly

Salt and pepper to taste

Set oven to 375ºF or Mark 5. Brush the pork rind with the oil and sprinkle lightly with salt. Place the joint on a rack in a roasting tin and cook for 30 minutes. Reduce the oven temperature to 350ºF or Mark 4 and cook for another hour. Cut the apples and pears into quarters and remove the cores, but do not peel them. Remove the roasting tin from the oven and drain off and reserve the fat. Place the fruit underneath the rack and pour in the cider. Return the pork and cook for another 30 minutes until the fruit is tender. Place the pork on a heated serving plate surrounded by the fruit. Measure the liquid in the roasting tin and make up to $^1/_2$ pint with water or stock. Measure 3 tablespoons of the reserved pork fat into a pan and stir in the flour and the Calvados or cider. Bring to the boil and simmer for 1 minute. Gradually add the stock and simmer for 2 minutes. Stir in the redcurrant jelly and season to taste. Serves 4.

Nut Cake

A rich cake that is chock full of nuts and flavour.

6 oz butter	½ teaspoon ground cinnamon
4 oz soft brown sugar	2 eggs, beaten
4 oz self-raising wholemeal flour	8 oz chopped hazelnuts or walnuts, or mixed

Set oven to 350°F or Mark 4. Grease and line a 7 inch square cake tin. Melt the butter in a pan over a low heat, stir in the sugar until it dissolves then remove from the heat and cool slightly. Sieve the flour and cinnamon into a mixing bowl, make a well in the centre and pour in the butter/sugar mixture. Add the beaten eggs, stir in the nuts and mix well. Put into the cake tin and bake for 30 to 45 minutes until golden brown. Test that a skewer inserted comes out clean. Cover with greaseproof paper if the top appears to be browning too quickly. Cool in the tin.

Elderflower Champagne

The white, frothy bunches of elder flowers have a strong perfume which infuses this sparkling, refreshing and easily made summer drink.

4 large heads of elderflower
(picked on a sunny July day)
1½ lb granulated sugar

2 pints boiling water
6 pints cold water
Juice and rind of 2 large lemons

2 tablespoons white wine vinegar

Do not wash the flowers, but remove any insects and the thick stalks. Place the sugar in a very large bowl and cover with 2 pints of boiling water. Stir until the sugar has dissolved. Then add 6 pints cold water, the rind and juice of the lemons, the vinegar and the elderflowers. Stir well. Cover and leave covered for 48 hours, stirring occasionally. Strain through a fine sieve into clean bottles with screw tops. Leave an inch gap at the top of each bottle and screw down well. Leave in a cool place to mature for 6 weeks but the champagne tastes better the longer it is left. Serve with ice if preferred.

Elderflowers and Irises *by Berenger Benger*

Harvest Time Pudding

An unusual sweet pudding from Lancashire containing carrots, potatoes and dried fruits.
Carrots add sweetness to the pudding and the mashed potatoes make it light.

4 oz self-raising flour	½ teaspoon ground mixed spice
4 oz fresh white or brown breadcrumbs	4 oz cooked mashed potatoes
	4 oz cooked mashed carrots
4 oz currants	2 oz dates, chopped
4 oz raisins	2 oz candied peel, chopped
Milk to mix	

Mix all the ingredients together very well in a large mixing bowl, adding just enough milk to make a soft dough. Put the dough into a large, buttered pudding basin and cover with greased greaseproof paper, then seal with kitchen foil. Make sure to fold a pleat in the centre of the paper and foil to allow the pudding to rise. Steam for 3½ hours. Serve with custard. Serves 4.

Plums with Port Wine

Ripe plums eaten straight from the tree can be the tastiest of harvest fruits and, baked with port and spices, they can be turned into a succulent dessert.

2 lb plums, halved and stoned   **8 fl oz port wine (or elderberry wine)**
4 oz soft brown sugar   **Pinch of freshly grated nutmeg**
Pinch of ground cinnamon

Set oven to 300°F or Mark 2. Place the plums in an ovenproof dish with a cover. Put the sugar and port into a saucepan and heat gently until the sugar dissolves. Then add the nutmeg and cinnamon and pour over the plums. Cover and bake for about 1 hour until the plums are tender. Serve either warm or chilled, with cream or yoghurt. Alternatively serve with slices of sand cake. Serves 6.

Haymaking by the Thames *by E. W. Haslehust*

Haymakers Beef

An old recipe for a rich, tasty stew, which was a favourite with haymakers.

2 lb stewing steak, cubed	**5 whole peppercorns**
1 onion, sliced	**Salt**
Bouquet garni	**3 fl oz wine or cider vinegar**
Pinch of ground cloves	**2 oz soft dark brown sugar**
Pinch of ground mace	**1 pint beer**

Place the meat and onions in a large bowl. Combine all the remaining ingredients, except the beer and pour over the beef. Cover and leave to stand overnight, turning the meat occasionally. Next day, tip the contents of the bowl into a large pan and pour in the beer. Bring to the boil, then reduce the heat, cover and simmer for 2 to 3 hours until the beef is tender. Remove the *bouquet garni* and serve. Serves 4.

Harvest Potato Pudding

A traditional supper dish, once eaten at the end of the potato harvest in Wales.

2 lb potatoes, peeled	2 rashers bacon, chopped
1 oz butter	1 onion, chopped finely
1 tablespoon flour	6 oz minced lamb, pork or beef
	Salt and pepper

Set oven to 375°F or Mark 5. Boil and mash the potatoes, then mix in the butter and flour. Fry the bacon, onion and minced meat until the onion is soft but not brown and stir into the mashed potato. Season to taste with salt and pepper and mix well. Turn into a greased pie dish and bake for about 20 to 30 minutes until the top is crisp and golden. Serves 4.

Cherry Tart

Really ripe cherries, harvested in July, make this delicious, open tart. For convenience, tinned cherries may be used but they will slightly lack the full, cherry flavour of freshly picked fruit.

Pastry: **8 oz flour   Pinch of salt   1 oz cornflour**
2 level teaspoons icing sugar   4 oz lard and margarine mixed
1 egg yolk   2 tablespoons cold water

Filling: **1lb black cherries, stoned (if using canned cherries, drain well)**
4 oz icing sugar   3 oz ground almonds
2 eggs   Almond essence

Set oven to 400°F or Mark 6. Sift the flour, salt, cornflour and icing sugar into a mixing bowl. Rub in the mixed fat and bind to a dough with the egg yolk and water. Knead the pastry lightly and roll out on a floured surface. Line a 9 inch fluted flan ring on a greased baking sheet with the pastry. Bake blind for 15 minutes. Reduce the oven temperature to 325°F or Mark 3. Arrange the cherries in the pastry case. Mix the icing sugar, eggs and almonds together with a little almond essence and pour the mixture over the cherries. Bake for 50 to 60 minutes until firm and golden. Serve hot or cold with cream.

Apple Cake

A simple, plain cake which is kept moist by the apple pieces.

8 oz self-raising flour	**4 oz caster sugar**
4 oz butter	**Grated rind of 1 lemon**
½ lb cooking apples,	**1 medium egg, beaten**
peeled, cored and diced	**2 oz sultanas (optional)**

Set oven to 375°F or Mark 5. Grease and line an 8 inch round cake tin. Put the flour into a mixing bowl and rub in the butter until the mixture resembles fine breadcrumbs. Stir in the apples, sugar, lemon rind and egg and mix well. Add the sultanas, if desired. Put the mixture into the cake tin and bake for 30 to 40 minutes until golden in colour and a skewer inserted comes out clean. Serve warm as a pudding with custard or cold, spread with butter.

A Harvest Home *by W. W. Quatremain*

Rose Hip and Honey Syrup

Diluted with cold water this syrup makes a pleasant drink and, being rich in vitamin C, with hot water it helps to keep colds at bay. Undiluted it can be used as a sauce for ice cream and for puddings.

4 lbs rose hips   9 pts water
Honey: 1 lb for every 1½ pints liquid

Bring 6 pints of the water to the boil in a preserving pan. Wash the rose hips and mince or chop finely in a food processor. Put them immediately into the boiling water, bring back to the boil, remove from the heat and leave to stand for 15 minutes. Then strain through a jelly bag and set aside the resulting liquid. Put the strained pulp back in the pan, bring the remaining 3 pints of water to the boil and pour over the pulp. Stir, leave for 10 minutes, then strain again. Put together both batches of strained liquid and measure the total amount. Return to the rinsed pan and add the appropriate amount of honey. Bring to the boil and boil for 5 minutes. Pour the syrup into hot, sterilised bottles and seal immediately. Use as required but store in a cool, dark place. Use dark bottles if available.

Pumpkin Pie

Many people assume this recipe to be American, but in fact it is English and dates from Tudor times. The early colonists introduced pumpkin to America where it quickly became a national dish, while here in England pumpkin fell from favour in the eighteenth century.

1 can pumpkin purée	**½ teaspoon ground ginger**
(450g approximately)	**¼ teaspoon grated nutmeg**
Pinch of salt	**2 eggs beaten**
4 oz soft brown sugar	**5 fl oz single cream**
1 teaspoon ground cinnamon	**8 oz shortcrust pastry**

Set oven to 375ºF or Mark 5. Grease an 8 inch pie dish or flan tin. Put the pumpkin purée with the salt, sugar and spices into a mixing bowl and combine together. Add the eggs and cream and stir well to mix. Roll out the pastry on a floured surface and use to line the pie dish or flan tin. Pour in the filling, spread out evenly and bake for 45 to 55 minutes until a knife inserted in the filling comes out clean. Allow to cool. Serve warm or cold with cream.

Pitching a Load *by George F. Nicholls*

Ham baked with Cider and Thyme

The farmer's wife and her helpers would bake an enormous ham for the harvest table.

3-4 lb boned and
   rolled gammon joint
2 onions, peeled and quartered
1 leek, sliced
1 stick celery, sliced
10 cloves

Parsley stalks
2 bay leaves
1 tablespoon chopped fresh thyme
4 oz Demerara sugar
4 oz Dijon mustard
½ pint dry cider

Soak the gammon in cold water for 12 to 24 hours if necessary, depending on how salty it seems. Place in a large pan, cover with cold water and bring to the boil. Skim off any scum. Add the onions, leek, celery, cloves, parsley, bay leaves and thyme. Cover and simmer slowly for 1½ hours. Set oven to 425°F or Mark 7. When cooked, place the gammon in a roasting tin and remove the skin, leaving the fat intact. Score the fat into diamond shapes. Mix the sugar with sufficient mustard to make a paste. Brush over the scored fat and bake for 35 to 40 minutes. Mix the remaining mustard and cider and baste the ham occasionally after the first 5 minutes. When the fat is golden, transfer to a warm plate and leave to rest for at least 10 minutes before carving. Serve hot or cold.

Harvest Betsy Cake

An early type of harvest cake, containing barley flour, which was widely used in days gone by.

8 oz barley flour	4 oz butter
8 oz white flour	4 oz caster sugar
1½ teaspoons baking powder	2 teaspoons black treacle
½ teaspoon salt	10 fl oz milk

8 oz currants or raisins

Set oven to 325°F or Mark 3. Grease and line a 7 inch round cake tin. Sift the flours, baking powder and salt into a bowl. Cream the butter and sugar in a mixing bowl until light and creamy and then beat in the treacle. Add the flour mixture and milk, alternately, until thoroughly incorporated, then gently fold in the dried fruit. Spoon into the cake tin and bake for 1½ hours or until a skewer inserted comes out clean. Cool in the tin for 15 minutes, then turn out on to a wire rack to finish cooling.

Soused Mackerel

The fishermen of Midlothian in Scotland celebrate their harvest from the sea with music and dancing in the streets and with this tasty dish.

4 mackerel, cleaned	**Salt**
5 fl oz water	**10 fl oz white wine vinegar**
4 bay leaves	**10 peppercorns**

Set oven to 300°F or Mark 2. Remove the head and backbone from each fish and roll up, skin side out, ending with the tail end. Secure each roll with a cocktail stick and pack the rolls tightly into a baking dish. Combine the rest of the ingredients and pour over the fish. Cover and cook for 1 hour. Remove from the oven, cool and keep the fish in the liquor in the refrigerator until required to serve. Serves 4.

Kentish Hop Pickers Cake

A lovely moist fruit cake which was carried out to the pickers in the hop gardens at teatime.

10 oz self-raising flour	**4 oz raisins**
1 teaspoon ground ginger	**4 oz sultanas**
1 teaspoon ground mixed spice	**2 oz candied peel, chopped**
$\frac{1}{4}$ teaspoon grated nutmeg	**15 fl oz milk**
6 oz butter, softened	**$\frac{1}{2}$ teaspoon bicarbonate of soda**
4 oz soft brown sugar	**1 teaspoon cream of tartar**

1 tablespoon black treacle

Set oven to 325°F or Mark 3. Butter and base line a 2 lb loaf tin. Sift the flour and spices into a mixing bowl and rub in the butter until the mixture resembles breadcrumbs. Stir in the sugar and fruit. Heat the milk to lukewarm in a pan and stir into it the remaining ingredients. Pour into the cake mixture and mix well. Put into the loaf tin and bake for about 1$\frac{3}{4}$ hours. Test with a skewer - it will come out clean when the cake is cooked. Remove from the oven and cool in the tin.

Hop Picking *by C. Essenhigh Corke*

Bacon and Cabbage

A favourite harvest supper dish in Ireland - simple and cheap.

1 cabbage   6 bacon rashers (or as many as may be preferred)
Lard or oil for frying

Shred the cabbage leaves finely and discard the tough stalk. Wash the cabbage and drain well then put into a pan with about half a cup of water. Cover and boil rapidly for about 5 minutes until the cabbage is almost tender. Drain the cabbage and dry in the saucepan, over a low heat. Fry the bacon rashers in the fat in a large frying pan until crisp. Remove from the pan and keep warm. Put the cabbage into the pan and cook in the hot bacon fat for a few minutes, turning the while. Pile the cabbage on to hot plates and top with the bacon rashers.

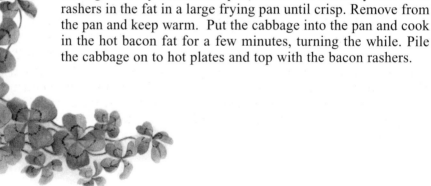

Summer Pudding

*This delicious and quintessentially English cold dessert consists of a bread lining
soaked with lightly cooked and juicy soft fruits.*

1-1½ lb fruit (a mixture of raspberries, strawberries, blackberries, blackcurrants)
Sugar to taste   **4-6 slices medium sliced bread**
Scant ¼ pint water   **5 oz whipped cream**

Take a 2 pint pudding basin, or soufflé dish. Cut the crusts off the bread and then
cut the bread to fit the base and sides of the dish. Put the blackberries and blackcurrants with sufficient sugar to taste into a pan with the water. Simmer gently until
almost soft, add the raspberries and strawberries and cook for a further 3 minutes.
Put the fruit mixture into the basin, reserving 2 to 3fl. oz of the juice. Top with the
remaining bread, pressing down firmly. Cover the basin with a plate or saucer to
fit the top exactly, place a weight on top and leave in the refrigerator overnight.
Turn out on to a serving dish just before serving and use the reserved juice to cover
any parts of the bread which have remained white. Serve with whipped cream.
Serves 4-6.

The Last Load *by Wilfrid Ball*

Lardy Cake

This rich cake was associated with pig rearing regions such as Wiltshire and was originally made using left over bread dough.

8 oz strong white flour	**$^1/_4$ oz fresh yeast**
$^1/_4$ teaspoon salt	**2 oz lard**
$^1/_2$ teaspoon ground mixed spice	**2 oz soft brown sugar**
5 fl oz warm milk	**3 oz raisins and sultanas (mixed)**

2 tablespoons water and 2 tablespoons caster sugar to glaze

Set oven to 450°F or Mark 8. Grease and line a 7 inch square cake tin. Sift the flour, salt and spices into a mixing bowl. Crumble the yeast into the milk and leave until frothy, then add to the dry ingredients. Mix to a soft dough, cover and leave to rise in a warm place for about 45 minutes. Roll out on a floured surface to $^1/_4$ inch thickness and spread with half the lard, sugar and fruit. Fold the dough into 3, turn to the left and roll out again. Repeat with the remaining lard, sugar and fruit. Fold and shape to fit the tin. Cover and leave in a warm place for 1 hour to prove. Heat the ingredients for the glaze in a small pan and simmer for 2 minutes. Score the top of the cake into diamonds and brush with the glaze. Bake for 30 minutes and test that a skewer comes out clean. Leave in the tin for 10 minutes then cool on a wire rack, spooning over any remaining syrup from the tin.

Stuffed Mushrooms

Large field mushrooms, freshly picked on an autumn morning will have more flavour, but shop-bought mushrooms will be quite satisfactory for this dish.

8 large, flat mushrooms approx. 4-5 inches dia.	4 oz wholemeal breadcrumbs
2 oz butter	4 oz Cheddar cheese, grated
1 medium onion, finely chopped	4 tablespoons chopped chives
	8 sage leaves, chopped

4 fl oz dry cider

Set oven to 400°F or Mark 6. Remove the stalks from the mushrooms and chop them. Melt the butter in a frying pan over a low heat, remove from the heat and use about half the butter to brush both sides of each mushroom. Arrange the mushrooms, dark side up, in a flat ovenproof dish. Soften the onion in the remaining butter then mix in the mushroom stalks. Remove from the heat, stir in all the remaining ingredients and pile the mixture on top of the mushrooms. Bake for 15 minutes and serve hot as a starter or as a light supper dish.

Harvest Cocktail

Before commercially made soft drinks were available, cordials were made at home. This simple recipe makes a refreshing drink.

2 oz oatmeal	**1 tablespoon warm water**
3 oz granulated sugar	**4 pints boiling water**
Juice of ½ lemon	**2 teaspoons ground ginger**

Put the oatmeal, sugar, lemon juice and warm water into a large pan and mix well. Pour in the boiling water and stir in the ginger. Bring to the boil and boil for 3 minutes, stirring constantly. Strain the mixture into a large jug and leave to cool. Serve chilled.

Hedgerow Jelly

A mixed harvest of Autumn hedgerow fruits can be preserved and enjoyed in this tangy jelly.

1 lb blackberries	**8 oz sloes**
1 lb elderberries	**Water**
1 lb crab apples	**Granulated sugar**

Prepare the fruit by washing it all and cutting up the crab apples roughly. An easy way to remove the elderberries from the stem is to put through the prongs of a fork. Place the fruit into a thick based pan and just cover with water. Simmer slowly until all the fruit is very mushy. Strain through a jelly bag - it is best to leave this overnight. Do not squeeze the bag or the resulting jelly will be cloudy. Measure the juice and place in a clean, thick based pan. Add 1 lb granulated sugar for each pint of juice extract. Stir over a gentle heat until the sugar has dissolved and then boil rapidly until setting point is reached; 220ºF on a sugar thermometer or test for set on a cold plate, when the jelly wrinkles. Pour into clean, warm jam jars and cover and seal in the usual way.

An Autumn Hedgerow *by Berenger Benger*

Pembroke Harvest Cakes

Simple snacks such as these fruited cakes were taken to harvest workers in the fields.

1½ lb strong white flour	**15 fl oz warm milk**
Pinch of salt	**3 oz soft brown sugar**
1 oz fresh yeast	**4 oz butter, melted**
	6 oz raisins

Set oven to 350°F or Mark 4. Grease baking sheets. Sift the flour and salt into a mixing bowl. Crumble the yeast into a little of the milk and stir into the remaining milk. When it is frothy add to the flour and stir in the sugar. Beat well and add the melted butter and raisins. Knead lightly, cover and leave in a warm place for about 45 minutes until risen. Turn out on to a floured surface and knead until smooth. Divide into 4 pieces and shape into flat cakes. Place the cakes on the baking sheets, cover and leave in a warm place for 15 minutes to prove. Mark each round into 4 with a sharp knife, separating the quarters slightly. Bake for 10 minutes then reduce the temperature to 350°F or Mark 4 and cook for another 25 minutes. Cool on a wire rack.

Cider Baked Pears

This simple recipe is a good way of using hard cooking pears.

1 oz soft brown sugar	**1 oz butter**
½ pint medium dry cider	**Clotted cream**
6 pears, peeled, cored and halved	**Chopped walnuts**

In a saucepan, dissolve the sugar in the cider, bring to the boil and cook for 5 minutes to make a syrup. Place the pears in an ovenproof dish with a cover and pour the cider syrup over them. Dot with butter, cover and cook for 30 to 40 minutes until the pears are tender. Cool and serve with clotted cream and a sprinkling of chopped walnuts.

The Watermill *by Wilfrid Ball*

Harvest Loaves

These saucer sized, scone-like loaves containing fruit and nutmeg were traditionally eaten by labourers working in the fields at harvest time.

1 lb self-raising flour	**1 oz sugar**
Pinch of salt	**2 oz currants or sultanas**
½ teaspoon ground nutmeg	**2 eggs, beaten**
4 oz lard	**Milk**
4 oz butter or margarine	**A little extra sugar**

Set oven to 375°F or Mark 5. Grease a baking sheet. Sift the flour, salt and nutmeg into a mixing bowl and mix well together. Rub in the fats until the mixture resembles breadcrumbs, then stir in the sugar and dried fruit. Add the eggs and mix with sufficient milk to form a soft dough. Turn out on to a floured surface, knead lightly then form into rounds, each about the size of a saucer. Place the loaves on the baking sheet with space in between, brush with a little milk and sprinkle a little sugar over. Mark the top of each loaf with a diamond pattern using a sharp knife and bake for 25 to 30 minutes or until golden. Makes about 4 loaves.

Blackberry Flummery

Flummeries, which are a form of blancmange, date back to medieval times, but were a particularly popular dessert in Tudor days. Other soft fruits, such as raspberries, blackcurrants, etcetera can be used in place of blackberries.

1 lb fresh blackberries, washed and any stalks removed

¹/₂ pint water	**4 oz sugar**
1 oz butter	**1 egg, separated**
1 oz flour	**1 teaspoon lemon juice**

Cream to decorate and boudoir biscuits

Cook the blackberries in a little water until soft, then sieve to produce a smooth purée. Allow to cool. Heat the ¹/₂ pint of water and the butter together in a saucepan until hot but not boiling, then remove from the heat. Mix the flour and sugar together and stir in to the pan, beating until smooth. Whisk the egg yolk into the mixture, return to the heat and cook, stirring, for 5 minutes; do not allow to boil. Stir the lemon juice into the blackberry purée and add to the mixture. Allow to cool a little. Whisk the egg white until it stands up in soft peaks and fold into the blackberry mixture. Turn out into a serving dish and chill well. Whip the cream until it stands up in soft peaks and pipe on to decorate. Serve with boudoir biscuits. Serves 4.

Damson Pie

*Damsons harvested from the hedgerows, together with orange and mace, give
this pie a rich, traditional flavour.*

Pastry:	8 oz wholemeal flour	2 oz lard
	1 teaspoon baking powder	3 oz butter
	Pinch of salt	4 tablespoons cold water
	Beaten egg to glaze	
Filling:	1 lb damsons	Pinch ground mace
	Grated rind and juice	4 tablespoons honey
	large orange	2 tablespoons tapioca or sago

First make the pastry and set aside in a cool place. Stone the damsons and put into a pan with the orange rind and juice, mace and honey. Set over a low heat, cover and cook gently for 15 minutes to become very juicy. Remove from the heat and mix in the tapioca or sago. Set aside and leave to cool. Set oven to 400°F or Mark 6. Roll out the pastry on a floured surface and use two thirds to line a deep 7 inch flan dish. Put in the damson mixture, cover with a pastry lid, seal the edges, brush with beaten egg and make a small steam hole. Bake for 30 minutes until golden brown. Serve hot or cold with whipped or clotted cream.

METRIC CONVERSIONS

The weights, measures and oven temperatures used in the preceding recipes can be easily converted to their metric equivalents. The conversions listed below are only approximate, having been rounded up or down as may be appropriate.

Weights

Avoirdupois	Metric
1 oz.	just under 30 grams
4 oz. (¼ lb.)	app. 115 grams
8 oz. (½ lb.)	app. 230 grams
1 lb.	454 grams

Liquid Measures

Imperial	Metric
1 tablespoon (liquid only)	20 millilitres
1 fl. oz.	app. 30 millilitres
1 gill (¼ pt.)	app. 145 millilitres
½ pt.	app. 285 millilitres
1 pt.	app. 570 millilitres
1 qt.	app. 1.140 litres

Oven Temperatures

	°Fahrenheit	Gas Mark	°Celsius
Slow	300	2	150
	325	3	170
Moderate	350	4	180
	375	5	190
	400	6	200
Hot	425	7	220
	450	8	230
	475	9	240

Flour as specified in these recipes refers to plain flour unless otherwise described.